ZZOO

THE

HORSE

EATS

NO

CUCUMBER

SALAD

ZOO

MA|DE

Published by **Palimpsest Press**
Edited by Jim Johnstone
Cover(s) + interior design by Obscure Design

LIBRARY AND ARCHIVES CANADA CATALOGUING IN PUBLICATION

TITLE: ZZOO / MA[vertical line]DE.
OTHER TITLES: ZZ OO
NAMES: MADE (Collective pseudonym), author.
DESCRIPTION: On the title page the author's name appears with a vertical line between MA and DE.
IDENTIFIERS: Canadiana (print) 20240527399 | Canadiana (ebook) 20240527496

ISBN 9781990293856 (softcover)
ISBN 9781990293863 (EPUB)

SUBJECTS: LCGFT: Poetry.

CLASSIFICATION: LCC PS8626.A3153 Z96 2025 | DDC C811/.6—dc23

Palimpsest Press would like to thank the Canada Council for the Arts and the Ontario Arts Council for their support of our publishing program. We also acknowledge the assistance of the Government of Ontario through the Ontario Book Publishing Tax Credit.

Canada Council for the Arts | Conseil des Arts du Canada

Canada

CONTENTS

WATER

LAND

TAXIDERMIA

WATER

"What would an ocean be without a monster lurking in the dark?" — **Werner Herzog**

MINIKIN

3

Our body, papered with chitin and shimmering
with scales, is skittish over open water.

We largely wander landwise, slinking
kitty-corner from winter's coming cold,
skirring southwest through a big sky.

Our body makes an exception for
the lake, where we flutter, reverent,

sipping nectar at the tip of a sweetwater sea,
waiting for the wind to touch our back

and guide us through

the open loch.

PITCHDOWN BAY

The small sound of a falling snowflake,
slow it down, low frequency rumble
of a whale, both melting into the ocean
in time, the water glowing as bright
as lanterns, and sailors drowning as if
they'd seen lighthouses, more lost men
entering from the shore's mouth, that
emptiness between the stars, pupils
compensating for this hard blanket of
deadlight night, still surrounded by
silent shorebirds, nested, watching,
stinging the surface of the water
like quickening nix when they alight.

THE EXTENDED MOURNING OF ORCA *J35*

like wailing in
whalesong   or waning
on a blue morning
the sea carries
sorrow for miles

do the fish hear
it like we do

mothered   for
seventeen months
before birth
orcinus   unnamed

of the realms
of the dead

alive

only for a
brief moment

behaviour set
adrift   through
perinatal space
the first phase
of grief lasts   for
seventeen days

pushing this shape

    the space between
droplets   a
body   of water
carried a thousand
miles
          rostrum
as a new womb

epimeletic
    until it is   pushed
          past the destiny
    of darkest
etymology

she waits   two
years   for a
third chance
at loss

VENTRAL

As above, this eternity below the ocean waves
is a bitter and frigid blue. Heavenly heads are
full of cold light, though blood swells their hearts
with auroras pink and gold.

Peaceful poison twinkles teal along the seascape,
winking at the passing sea angels whose wing-fins
flutter like twin flames, flare pinpoints of holy
fluorescence.

Lucid as water, naked as an androgynous body,
their interior intimacy is brightly exposed, tweaked
into the devilish curl of buccal cones. Free-floating,
slow-moving alongside the drift ice,

violence graces the angels. They crush butterflies
in the dusk of the midnight zone, gorging their young,
who will swell like a red wave until they overwhelm
the bodies that bore them.

BLUE SUNLIGHT

The tent was an island, rooted in a bitter sea.
Sometimes, it's better to be sweet,
but others, the dark greens are the only ones
that will grow, so we grind them between
our teeth, or fluff them to cover the ground.
Fuel and blood and water and milk
all spill the same way but only one
will stoke a fire. Black is

an absence

or is it a harbinger; it takes you in,
feather of a corvid's wing used to write
here in the sand, an X for anyone to find.
Lost senses pulse or lull alongside —
everything else, just horizon.
Restless, we blue the sky together.
The sea is jealous of those who
don't swallow their treasures.

FAMILIAR

In a wild country

invocations
become invitations.

Voices: trilling,
croaking

spilling into full,
ineffable bloom:

precious jewels
inside the head crystallize

against doom-tickled scum
lip-synced into
creek, meadow, pond.

They scavenged me once,

neck closed
eyes closed

this wand, these swords
flying inside
another frog's

inverted spleen

where words splay
and wards raise.

Apotropaic shroud against
the archaic plague

of locusts rising

vague as mushroom bells
of gloom-grey cloud:

crossing the pocky terrain
between
tempest & restraint,

the tocky earth turns
to incandescent plane.

When all of nature
feels incantatory *I leap*
I greet

to offer milk & meat,
bed down sweet in lamb's wool.

We will be tongue-tied
by affinity,

running the rhythms
of our own cunning cadence.

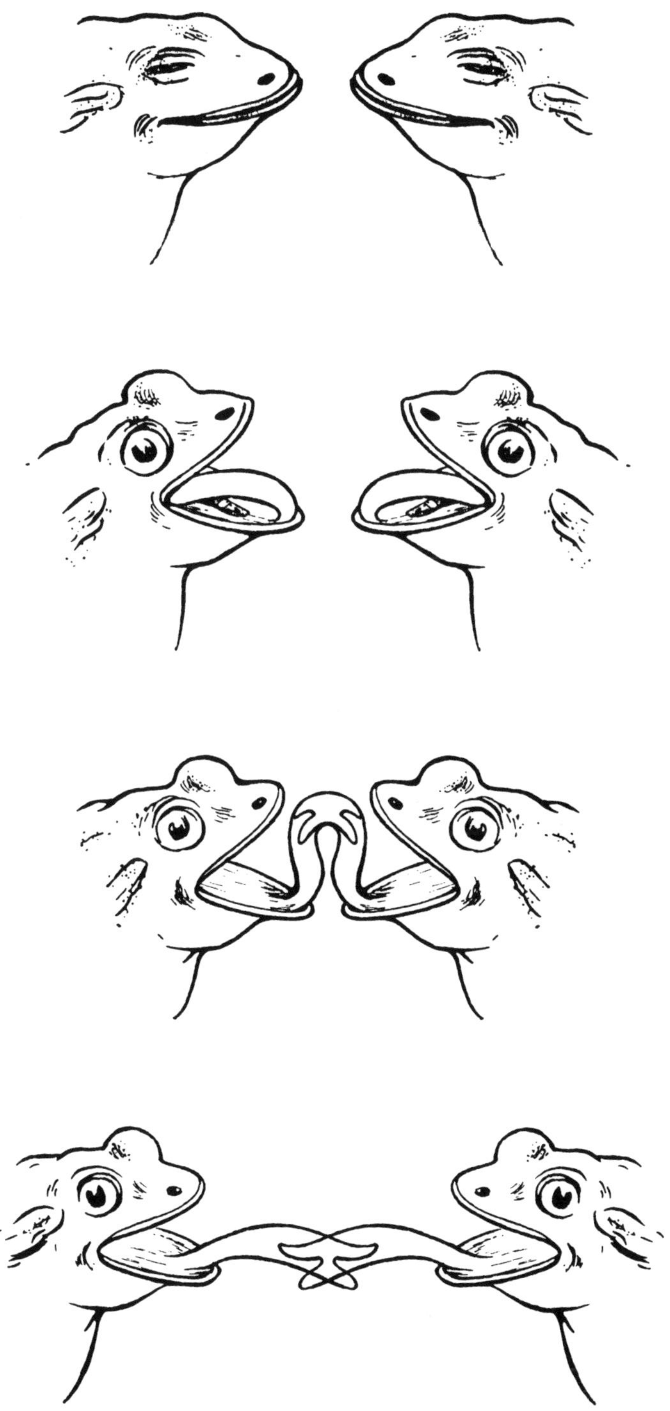

THEY EAT THEM WEEPING

Crocodiles are known for their insincere tears, but alligators are better conduits for both sorrow and joy. Their closed-mouth, lemon-lime grins leak teeth everywhere, a terror barely contained. Sealed jaws drop, bending paths into slow rivers. *Snip-Snip* tickles skins, hisses at hallucinogens, hunts downwind from the accidental moments that provide the splash-sweet tuck of life. A dainty morsel awaits, so fish or cut bait — it's time to take arms by the orange groves then rehydrate in the heat. Crocodilians are not unlike dogs, sun-sprawled in mud or dust, mouths spread gleefully to catch whatever resembles a comestible. Someone is coming through the gate. *Wally* and *Albert* surface at night, when stars peep and moon creeps. Saurian hunger is a thirst, baited with the fruit of human cruelty. Huff. Civilization is a very thin veneer, a drop in the swamp to regret later.

NARCOMEDUSA

I long to kiss your thin wrists,
to shake weight until you are thrown
down thick and grinning. Limb or
phantasm, fading into someone else's life.
Your teeth leave a soft smile of bruises
that lasts for days after you've gone.

Cotton ball bunny, we'll baby our wounds
with ice cubes and alcohol, ACE bandages
and acetaminophen. Antiseptic ticking,
time blooms a rose to mark the unjaded way
pleasure bursts forth from pain.

Taste yourself.

Sour candy and vodka on your tongue,
electric lollipop sparking against your braces.
Lip stretches away from lip, a new life form,
a jellyfish no one thinks will sting.

INTERDOMINION

Wolf spider crawls, calm and cold,
eight relentless legs spiking through
a frozen world. Spilled ink on thin ice.

She hunts in snowy darkness on
the lid of the lake; her hunger a duet
with the universe, always demanding

attention. This crystal land, impassable
in summer, feels distant as an aphelion
beneath her tarsi. Low light motion

vibrates in her periphery, seen directly
and indirectly across the perils of this
sparkling architecture; she moves to it.

Like a severed hand scratching at
a mirror, she pounces. Fingers clasp
at clear ice, deflected. Envenomed.

Through the glassy gap, an unblinking
eye observes. Viscous shape shimmers
below, floats nebulous. Subtended

tentacle mirrors spider's electric touch,
tapping up gently at the frosted lid.
A refractive pause. Infinity between.

VORTEXT

Lake Michigan is a clamorous collector, accumulating sailors beneath
its trenchant freshwaters; a lepidopterist, pinning planes by their wings to the benthic zone; a dioramist,
holding its shapeshifted mysteries vitrined in bathyspheric hideaways. It swallows, setting ships down on beds of shale,
then gulps, garlanding them in coral and barnacles, replenishing
their cabins with fish. Its dramatic vanishings triangulate the space connecting Ludington
to Benton Harbour to Manitowo, a temperamental false mirror whose glassy stare holds the power to
inflict catastrophic misfortune on the warm meat and
metal peregrinating overhead. Small surface creatures, resisting submersion,
attempt to fathom loss. They drag the lake with sonar, map the speculative sites
of shipwrecks past; a history of abnormal
incidents that will offer no satisfactory explanations, only
the allure of fragments and light debris. Even Mishigami's mile
of ancient herding stones must
be kept secret from a crude or fussy public
who is breathless to chase the hearsay of any
leviathan's vicious,
talespinning sparkle …

CRYOCAESURA

the wheel
turns the
hibernator
wakes up
shedding
sheets of
frost biting
the skin
below the
ice shelf
far from
sunlight
an expanse
bigger than
ourselves
deep inside
a drill hole
tunnels in
a warming
world life
revivified
from its dim
dreaming
the machine
within now
breathing
through
the lines

LAND

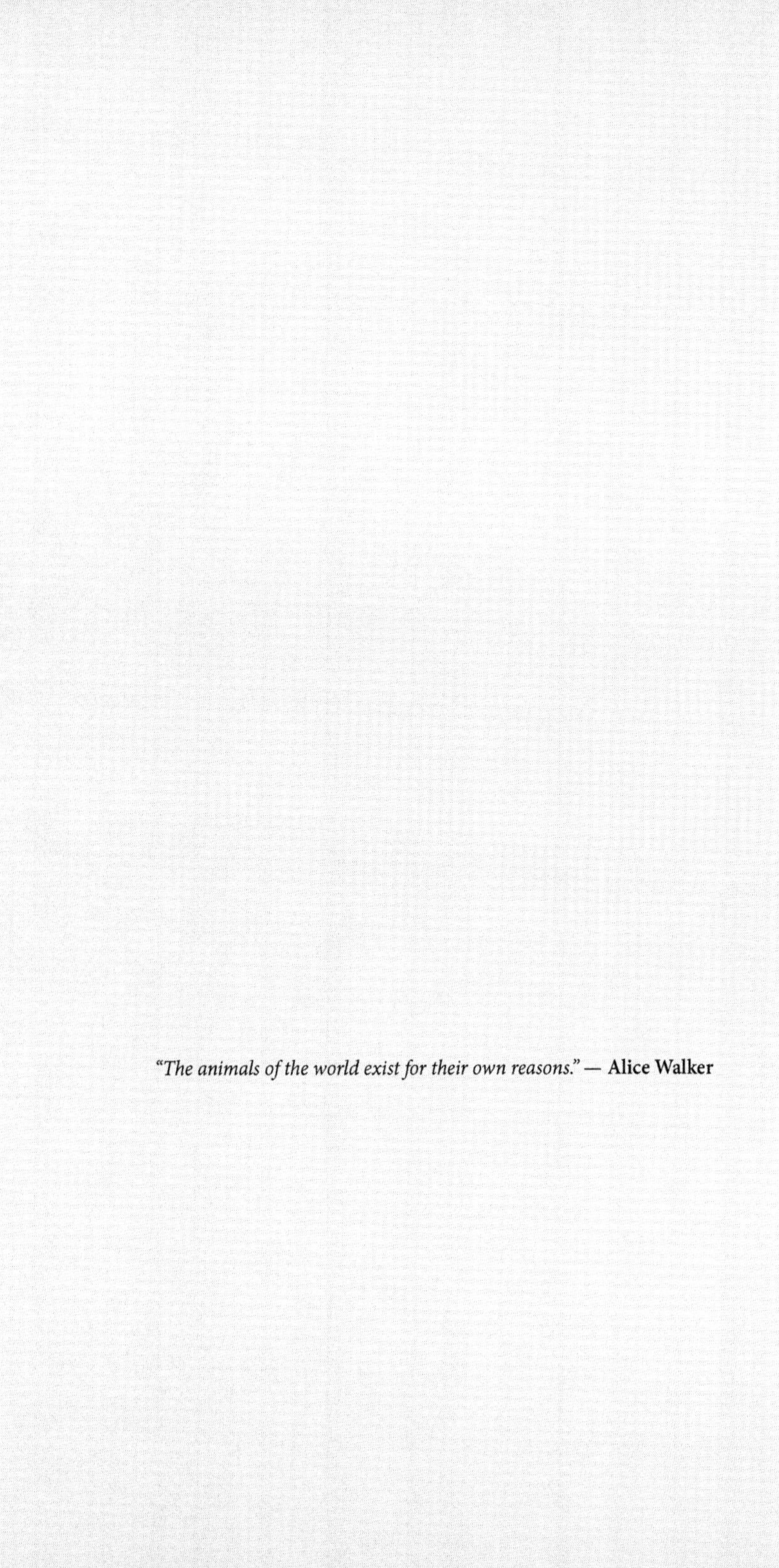

"The animals of the world exist for their own reasons." — **Alice Walker**

MILKWEED

1

What we devour is who will be

Our body moves   along   its path
                                        it grows

We eat fresh   nibble
          eat bitter   chew
                    eat continuously   gnaw
and   swallow

swallow

          swallow

If we are not taken by bird
snake or spider   we grow
                              exponentially

                                        burst out of skin
                                        show stripes

eat and crawl
eat and swallow

                              phasing through five instars

bodies green-yellow
to dotted white

brimming with biting
cardenolide

inheriting the toxins sucked from
the leaves of silky
swallow-wort our waystation
our ghastly angel

We gorge monotrophic
and do not give back

consume the season's tender shoots
pitilessly

leave it to the honeybees
to scatter
pollen over the fields

When we've had our fill
our mandible will shut itself deliciously

while spinnerets move to churn
the silk of dissolution

AS THE NEXT DAY DAWNED

The opening crawl broke:
Sequenti die aurora apparente …
Panic lives wild outside city walls,
born extreme to marginal land.

When the goats in their coats of cobalt
and alabaster rise, forelegs thrown back
like wings, hind canons carrying their
weight, they are luminaries.

Formed wrong, but stubborn as a blaze
between the horns, they pay no mind
to their quadruped spines, find the
balance of the barely possible.

Alert to the rhythm of morning,
this hunger to move is always vanward,
a guarded march through aubade that
refuses to obey the covenance of matter.

We bear them on beds of red ribbon
and straw, diagram their angles on
upended stars, let them scale the ash tree,
unwholly elevated, to eat of its leaves.

We have survived a decamillennium beside
their kind, waiting for an upright rarity to
tell us how to turn failure, phantom of all
terrors, into the kindling of their cynosure.

WHEN WE WERE WOLVES

If you look long enough at trees
you will become one. A wolf chews
bark in its garden of Eden: to salivate
at the sound of a bell, to get to the ataraxia
of knowing exactly what comes next.
Howling is another kind of cooing;
now is the only time it ever encounters.

These teeth belong outside,
under the rib cage of a small animal.
Snow static, faded bunny rabbit,
cottontail her in the thick dry leaves.
Body like thorns with welded seams.
Blushing red, rarebit blanket
that dreams may nest in.

Whatever is left of her will tremble
in the blow of detritivores, resurface
on the back of a mushroom whose
rhizomes have grown across acres.
Even the lifeless are only briefly still.
If you look long enough at rocks,
you will notice they also become trees.

MENAGERIE

Pillow, chrysalis, claw:
you wake, locked inside

a Walkerville two-story.
Time has made you wild,

a captive inside your taxonomic
home. The scenery outside

is flutteringly alive, stirring
behind tableau curtains.

The skies are *severe clear*
and there are bars clouding

your head, a manifestation
of today's migraine or else

a protection annexed onto
a messy world. Sugar glass

comfort for a gilded cage,
catch yourself spitting into

the fishbowl, putting key to
locket. Screens go masking

to distract the eye, meshed
up tight to keep the time flies

buzzing. Maybe it would be
better to be a weed in a wild

field but you are more like
a blue rose flocked by delicate

avian darlings, nibbling on
the crusts of fickle patronage.

A chain link fence defines the yard,
plucked raw and tilled turf green.

This is a boundary that the furred
or feathered don't see, one your

neighbours will help watch in
the middle of the hooded night.

Culture is a strange beast,
a petri dish of cells on display.

A zoo is a garden where animals
grow, to make space for the city.

NO PERFORMANCES TODAY

At *Showmen's Rest,* first-class boneyard for circus shellbacks, the whistling past turns over, a dirty signal pulling at the lingering quiet. A handful of blinked-out stars from the firmament reside here, eighty-six conjoined souls buried in a Big Top grave. Those who stumbled through their days now tuck away in the wailing night, silent. Clowns who always entered the ring with their right feet first, acrobats who never whistled under canvas tents, strongmen who eschewed peanuts in their dressing rooms, all clutching at kernels that did not protect them; they share a final act. The pranksters that made the world gasp, who vowed to chase more laughter than tears, were undone in their sleeping cars, in the predawn, at Ivanhoe Interlocking, where Life slipped on a banana peel. A dead-heading train tore into them from behind, snatching up the tumblers and fire-eaters, ringmasters and tightrope walkers. A hot, buttery end full of steam and kerosene. No animals were harmed. Out of the gates of death, that universal cage, came the coterie of bears and hippopotamuses, giraffes and rhinoceroses. Carrying the show for the signal tower. Now, in the necropolis, the grandstanders and roustabouts are silent for the first time, as stone elephants step into the caretaker's enormous shoes. Trunks sunk low, sifting the grass, they configure a vigilant ring, genuflection for those who bowed out. Crowds, parading their grief, come bearing the world's cotton-candy condolences.

DEATH GOES GREEN

One species' trash is another's
sustenance, this is the paradigm
of all endurance. Endings in
unended landscapes. An ant

responds to its hill, feeding a colony
with crumbs. The sky above looks
bigger today. Absence will do that
to a space, like when fungus absorbs
plastic into itself. But death has always
been green, its bone roots reaching,
pushed into living soil.

Escape from Trash Mountain, so many
unmade things. The bears play dead;
an old tree falls and they pretend not
to hear it. Close their eyes to the night
and make the moon disappear.

Garbage is never ugly in the dark.
The moon does not exist if nobody
is looking. It goes out like a snuffed
candle when the sun blinks.

PYTHON SKIPPING ROPE

You might be as gentle as a gorged
python, but I crush like a common boa.

We form a cordon, create waves,
swiftening circle of lapping;
fresh danger will only escalate
these imbricating desires.

Tongues spiral, sweep past one another.
Show me your fangs and I will break
the tips to make a point.

Alone together, sticky and pretty,
our vulnerabilities rake along
the ground. Whispers in dirt.

Tessellations of peacock feather
freckle with rain to aid in camouflage,
then fan the flames of roughness
and love, a braid we cannot undo.

VORESCAPE

Cold could not touch him in
the winter cave, sleeping between

wolf bodies, listening to
the clicking bats overhead.

It comes for him now,
vile dog or hungry idea, finding

the cracks in his cottage
walls. Whistling through gaps in

the teeth of village men: they laugh
because he is praxis but not politic.

His doctor says, *Laugh back —*
everyone knows less than you.

Some mornings he looks
backward, ardently mourning

the forest, that pack he left behind.
The dogs he recalls are long dead,

their lot replenished by new generations
who would not recognize him

as a creature

who once belonged to them.
The use of costume as camouflage

is a ruse that only works on humans.
Cologne and woollen sport coats

are long shadows shorn across
the torsos of men, thin garments

perfectly inconspicuous in
the street, achingly gawdy in

the woods.

When he was young, he blamed
the wolves for his disappointment

with humanity. His mother died,
his father ran, a stranger left him to tend

a herd of goats. He thought that was just
the way life went, until a twig snapped,

the luna wolf curled around him
and her pups gave up pieces of

their meat.

As his seventh decade ends, his
sentiment changes — he sees how he might

have come to hate winter indoors, or his
parents' natural weakenings, regardless.

What remains for him now, but to rip
the skin along its perforation,

reveal

the interior landscape — let
the bones shake with joy.

SPLICE / STITCH

Leap ahead, go
straight to the end:

you can replicate a gene but
you can't step in a river twice.

Words erase the possibility
of your future reproduction.
Pre-uterine maze; *largo*.
By anatomy alone, you'll keep
on forgetting, collecting,
knowing that what
awaits you is loss.

A tear in the hide is
widened by a panicked flight.
Blood on the leaves seems
a longer trail for death to follow
than lying in the pool of a clearing.

Wounded deer, broken helix, gutted
lamb, remember: *lose* is not *lost*.

Stay not, say still not.

ORGANON UNRAVELLING

This stomach thrums through
knots, everything chasing anything.
Cut out the organ and hang it on the wall
next to the rug-hooking of a liger.

Thrust into the trust,
spit-tickled domestic felicity.
I don't know whether to laugh
or take you, call you, home.

This concept is a skeleton, an arm
turning the crank of its own *vanitas*.
Glaze the stilled bones straight;
death is posterity made perfect.

Skin is misleading; once in it, we rust pretty.
Wake up one day, too old to make anyone
look good in my leather. I apologize
but you'll never know why.

ZOOMORPHS

We believe we have subdued
the brute animalism within us;
that the lizards of our basal ganglia
have been caught in a maze
of neomammalian complexity;
that the hoary Minotaur is
wandering the labyrinth, waiting
to be killed; that Moreau's beast folk
forebode a hybrid hypothesis
we have been wise to avoid.

A creature sleeps beneath
the Janus mask of our civility.

This is the tenet we share with
our other kin, our collective subset
of fundamentalist furries. Theriotype
stereotypes fashion their animuses
into cottony suits, costumes to wear
in place of all too human flesh.
Frisky dingoes and curious kittens
illuminate the metaphysics
of plushophile lust.

But there, in the thick hair of our
bodies, the flagrancy of our defensive
fangs, the herds of us shouldering

against the cold world, it is clear
as a bell jangling from a collar:
our superstrata are semi-feral
as well.

Nuzzle our wet-nosed traumas,
lick at our scratched realities.
Lean into our fingernails scritching
on one another's backs; our gentle
hands on the horn of a unicorn;
our serpents at the breast.

Marrow to epidermis,
every layer of us is pet.

FURVERTS

Who is prepared to wait to be properly
reincarnated, or gene-tugged into
the future?

Not us.

We take the world up, sew it closer
to the pattern of our desires,
cloth bright as a cartoon.

We come into this new zoo
through the closet, type: *open door,*
escape to safer spaces.

Spellbound and hounded in
another Saturday night
masquerade,

our chrysalis of
youth is continually

unfolding,

tuning against
the dull pulse of terrene.

A hamster is running rampant
across the keys. Read the text

that spools across the screen,
human words in bestial mouths:

They're Gr-r-reat!

Feeding on milk-soaked
anthropomorphic dreams,

we'll go looking
for each other

out where the internet
never ends.

The impermanent house
has been tented, wrapped
in muffled cloth

swallowed alive
by some huge animal.

We shiver
in our fun fur

sniff at inner flesh
exposed to air, stroked by
knowing paws,

joy's dirty tail
thumping the floor.

This libidinal churn,
a ripple of the coat, is lust

sidling up to innocence.

Questions fuzz like dust
bunnies along the edges
of ever changing rooms.

We're pooling our fantasies,
low poly sprites in a garden
of prismatic light.

When skin crawls and minds
purr, we bump against

the immovable
body

of a tree inside a forest
of illusion.

Zip up the mascot:

when the heart is happy,
the strawberries turn red.

THE TAIL

Worst of all, he wasn't funny.
But then, neither was I, always starting
with a punchline.

It's fine for today to be a tickle.

When I hand him tomorrow's newspaper,
baneful and grey as the sky before rain,
he'll still be querying laughter.

Sun in the eyes:
                    happiness is glaring.

Laughter is a sublimation of pain. The crowd
does not give its applause; this joke never quite
worked, did it? But we go on, a little shaggy,

unsure of what genre we are performing.

AIR

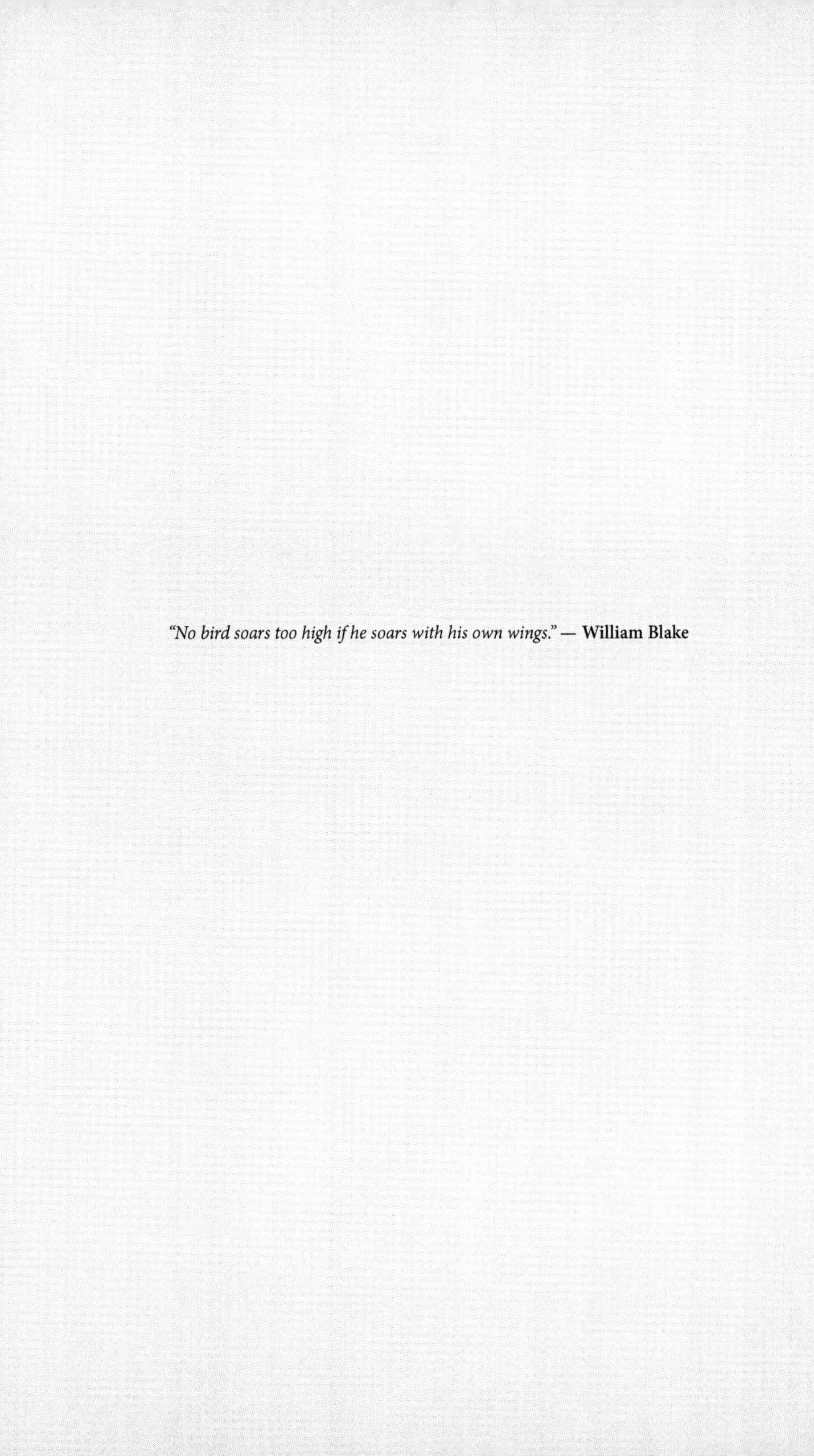

"No bird soars too high if he soars with his own wings." — **William Blake**

MICHOACÁN

4

Wings, wind-kissed,   patterning us into
a slow listen;
            no destination,
                        only direction.

Like a dizzy leaf high on air, we are free-
flowing from there to here, flowering

through fields and neighbourhoods all
across the continent.

                        Gathering swarm,
millions of monarchs navigate in silence,
take a lipless read of a solar compass.

Moving southwest in autumn
across migration's invisible map:

                                    edging inland from
                                    the Atlantic,

                ridged by
the Rocky Mountains,

                                        curbed by
                                    the Caribbean,

we are siphoned toward the unknown; our
instinctual pilgrimage, a chaos program …

Like a hurricane, we spill across three
countries, kaleidoscope over thousands of

miles, to return to a place we have never seen.
Against chance, we arrive in the cloud forest,

among the Oyamel firs
of Michoacán,

their branches massive
against our delicate grams.

Roosted by the ton, folded bodies cluster
like dry leaves.

We close tender eyes
and tired wings,

drink this damp and sacred air,
the breath of trees,

warming to our
diapause.

VERTICAL LOGIC AT THE CROSSROADS OF THE WORLD

When my French exit meets your *l'esprit de l'escalier*,
                        a door is left open between us.
Whose feet will move through that gaping mouth first?
I'm done with doubt but you will still always doubt that;
so I hope for you to call me back
and you wait for the return of my goodbye.

The first time was in the middle of a thunderstorm.
There was a party, so I forgive you, I guess,
for letting me wreck my velvet in the rain,
for the fact that when I left,
only the wet rook had anything to say.

There was no turning back. Our sweetness
was wind-whipped, lost in a kiss blown south.
We waved away the taste, wasted the light.
I should have stood you under flinty stars.
You should have forked a socket into my mouth.

FLASHBACK TO THE CRAB NEBULA

In the library, I find a book left backwards,
pages turned into a blackout.

Tomorrow you will hear a bird downtown
with a whistle like mine.

Memory reverberates throughout a life:
wide, white. When we notice it, it dazzles,

dying light of a star that cannot make crops grow,
loved only by the lonely cowboys sleeping beneath it.

And still we are driven to explore: small fires burn bright;
what are you supposed to do when you see the flash?

Split the night open and crawl into it,
a sleeping bag you have carried all day.

SUBSIDIZED HOUSING FOR SMALL BIRDS

Start right now, build regardless of the season. Every little nest needs a bird. Work to make it look like it all grew there naturally.

Delight the sapsuckers and they will reward with frequent visits. Should this fail, don't feel too badly. Few flyers survive their first year, and there are other kinds of success.

Whether songbird, or kestrel, we recognize their timbre, their particular chitter & whine. Shrill keys fall on sharp ears.

One oriole ate wheat. Swore off the opulence of fruit nectar & insects. A protest against the coming of the suburbs.

We had to give up on goldfinches. The birding hotline was overrun, its tape exhausted by reports of commonplace marvels.

If there are starlings, look closely at the night sky. Anything worth seeing is worth photographing, exposed by the light of the moon.

See the reflections of trees & sky in the glass, windows of detuned opportunities. Flickers go out with the light.

A lost iPhone vibrates against a hummingbird song. Tweets resurface, echoing through the forest until someone is there to hear them.

A scratched throat revolts. Here we go again, arguing about sound poetry with screech owls. This contact call has gone cold, won't be answered.

It's summer. Look out the kitchen window: mourning doves with bent wings will require treatment, or tears. We must be aware of the land we are dealing with.

Skeptics are breaking open eggshells to see what's inside. Robins discard the gaunt, abandon the angular and wait for the rest.

When grey skies delimit
bluejays, our last careless
hold on warmth is lost.
Lovers will come home
bearing roadkill.

The frames of our houses come
from the torsos of their trees.
We replant twin sycamores, single
poplars, forming their roosting
boxes in the image of our own.
We hold out our hands, brimming
with sunflowers & sorghum,
say *it's for the birds.*

MINIMAL SURFACES

Never get your hands dirty
with someone who can buy better soap.
Split inconsiderate
                                        in half; boil it down
in human tears. Fat in toxic glycerine.

Listen, it's glistening: ejaculating glitter.
Forget your rich friends!
I'll show you the decadence
money wishes it could buy.

Lonely tylenol disturbs metabolism;
this is an attempt at a cleanse.
The liver does not quite agree
and thinks you should stop subjecting it
to the peer review of detox juicing.

Palms down on honey onyx,
beeswax burning into ginger serenity,
you can't remember the last time you were
in a garden. Maybe it was the day after your
grandmother died fifteen years ago, when
you stood beneath her lemon tree.

Is this your freshly soured story,
the claw that you refuse to wash clean?
Taste this fruit, a bubble in your mouth.

PANOPTICONDOMINIUM ®

Panopticondominiums,
man's new plants, sown
straight as grapevines.
Those who didn't see you
get fucked last night
heard about it later.

Shoulder to shoulder,
coffin-wide, to exit excited.

The future doesn't really want
to get built; sometimes you just
have to force it. You don't really
want to live in aeries, communicating
through elaborate tin cans.

But you do want to be watched,
checked for insecurities.

Even the ceiling fans have eyes here.

When you hear whispering
it is never to you but only about you.
Alone on the ninth floor, you listen to
the hourly knock upon the window and
think *the ravens never fly this high.*

ARBEITSLIED

when the steel rises and the voice of

the labouring world hums, cortisol

levels elevate   when a noisy truck

rattles by, we duck and cover   when

a car alarm dents the air,

it uncaws a crow and dream booms into

all our animal heads   when the streets

sing, the sparrows in the branches of

the boulevard trees do not   when

power lines hum and rubber makes

music on concrete, the chorale is

overwhelmed with new polyps,

the colours bleed into one another and

old melodies suffer   when the airplanes

roar, the seasons cease to speak

and tree crickets struggle to recall

the canticles they used to dance to,

their affinity reduced to a bumbling

two-step   when ships pass and

infrasound insists, humpback whales

hold elephants in their mouths, waiting,

while the chambers of the sea

look on without remark

APOCALYPSE PARROT SCREAMS FOR VENGEANCE

Grey parrot, white noise, sky gone black / hearing the Master's voice while answering / Sunken head trained full of dread / like a horn tester in a car factory / Screech or whine, swaying & screaming / Death growl, glossolalia / *Malum in se*, its outburst / Open throat exposed, it runs under drones / This animal moaning anarchy, an orchid verbalized / Syrinx, column of air, floral nectar / Distortion's dream, feather-pummelled / Riding on Death's shoulder to bite at your ear / *Membrana tympaniformis*, its mimicry / Nest intense, winged speed spreads / A velvet loon is a glittering foil to overcome / These voices are caged by slight bones / on an island of instability / Words twist, get carried away

SKY BIRD

When the clouds took human
shape, we felt indivisible; heaven

and body, ontology as a single plane,
brittle pane. Arms out, embracing balance.

When the clouds looked like
lambs, we laid down our heads.

The cabin blanketed us in filtered air,
a leisurely middle space that transcended

the clamour of cities, the buzz of insects.
The double-bind of moving forward

while sitting still sent us daydreaming,
as short-lived as contrails scattered

on a path across the chameleon blue.
We coasted past imperceptible longitudes

and borderlines, riding the edge of
the lower stratosphere. Between the rest

of our lives and where we are now —
this is the distance we always hoped for.

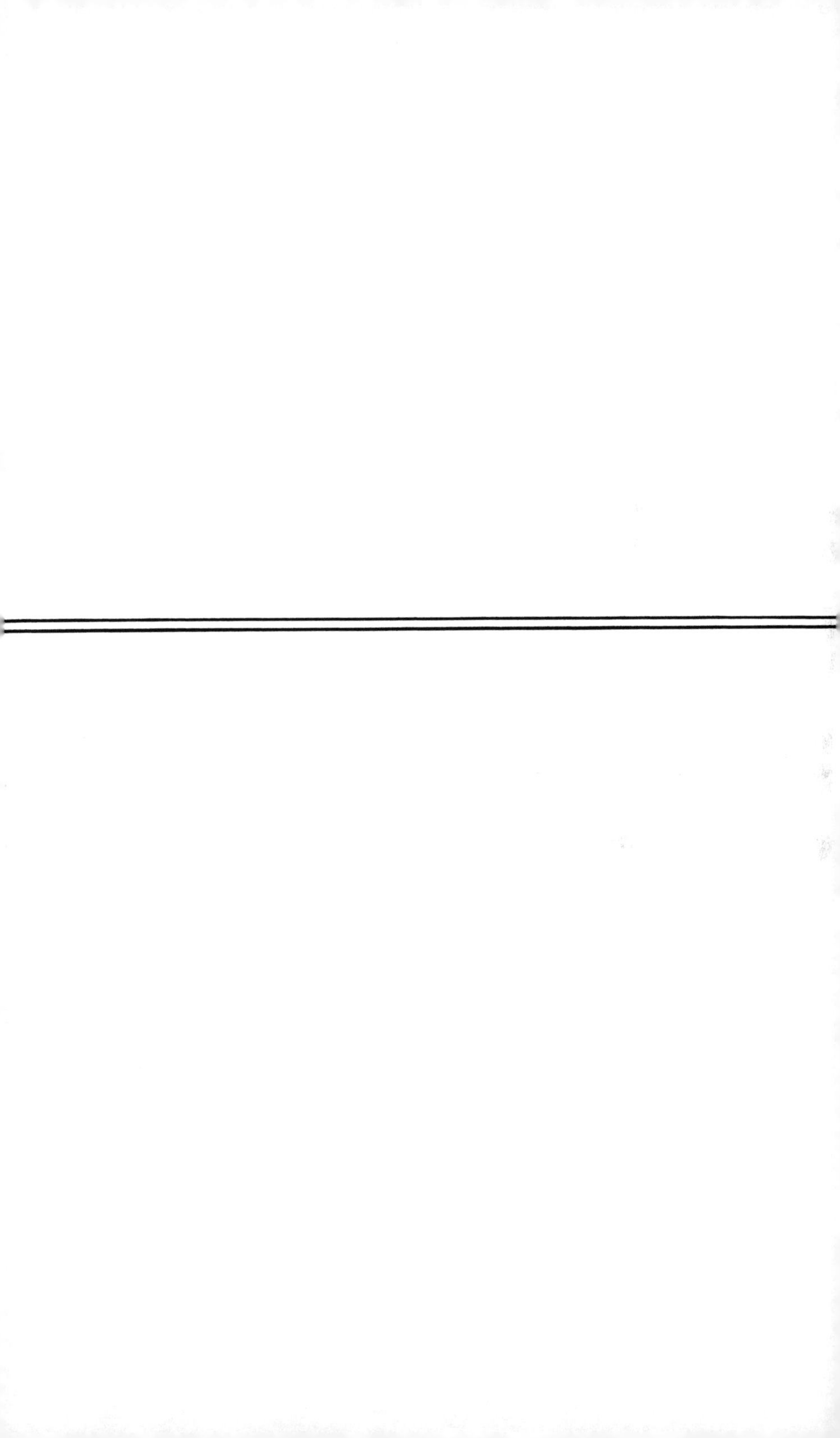

ELSEWHERE

"Even the smallest of creatures carries a sun in its eyes." — **Antonio Porchia**

METEMPSYCHOSIS

2

Still earthbound; spin a silk mat
to cling to.

After the final split,
our striped skin hardens into a chrysalid shell
                                                                                    to shelter us.

We must pull an eidolon
from the universe, turn loose

          the storm cocooned within us.

Air comes through a hundred fine
filament tubes, piercing
          the matrix
                                        of this umbilical world.

A catalytic force breezes in,

one part death, lick of an afterlife,
soul extract making its presence felt
                                                                                in these shifting cells.

Each adaptation is a correction:

we are compounding eyes
                    reordering organs   fleshing out
                                                 fresh muscles,

                              building the homunculus
                                    of another life.

Our body is pushed through
many versions of itself. What melts away

          reforms,
          resolves

into Müllerian mimicry, a shared language
of poison mapped along black borders,
in radiant orange and delicate yellow.

Our rise consumes the soul's glassy waste,
tickles it out of existence.

When the time is right
we emerge transformed,

thrash our wet and crumpled
wings until we are free.

NERVE BOUQUET

And then there was the outbreath;
milk blue marble in an empty hallway.
A spiral staircase rings ouroboros.
Under threat, the body eats its unshed cells,
Moebius-stripping itself to death.

Upsy-daisy, glitching in a hoopla cry.
The system, having quarantined a virus,
resets. Chrome spiderwebs on the windows
in the fiction of grey matter; if this circulatory
system were more of a circuit board,
medicine might work. If this ambit
were an abyss, it could never be mined.

One day, even this loop of fingers
will be impossible, but I will still
slither into the gyre of your hand, or turn
to honeysuckle, twining around
your slack knuckles.

SUGARWHIP

First the stick:

and we are stuck, wind-up animals
balking at the claw, as though,
if we move slowly enough, we can
suspend the progression from egg to
super-predator, as though we might
sidestep the slippery, spiraled future,
which carries the threat of our own
genetic dearth, rich disturbance
in the slush, our grunting,
sturdy resistance to blackthorn
twig dissolved across distances,
hooves deep in mud, tendrils
crittering along the double-helix
twist of our next skin, aware of
nothing except the concentrated
drag of movement in the trees

Then the carrot:

crucial, sweet, fatted like a trap,
a pleasure to tickle gill or throat,
to distract us from the imbalance of
power, for Earth is the single apex,
the only alpha, a thunder that will
swallow us like an afterthought,
except for our fullness, which grows
with each growl, heat hiccupping
from thorax into waveform, vorous
rasping of the animal inside the
intestine, the noise of our wheels
turning as we purr between the
carcass, mutating to stave off
death, warming into this restless,
divergent future, always choosing
the brightest, most edible ending

WRECKED BY A CLOUD

Lost in the wilderness of everyday life:
Would you mind if I tagged along with you?
Happily derailed by someone else's dream,
it is a long way down when you are wrecked
by a cloud. My only desire, freckled with rain.
Shoulders shaped by tension, letters cramped
like the closeness you are still hoping for.
The river does not always lead us to civilization,
sometimes it only takes us to the edge
of the fathomless sea. A briefly experienced
eternity.

PSYCHOPOMP

When I found you, underfed and wanting,
you were sheltered in a holding cell,

an *Animal Sola* in urban scrubland.
I was the same, but uncaged,

a fallen giant who, then and there,
swore myself to you and your thereafter.

That afternoon, bit by the grey frost
of February, I yielded to the rare luxury

of a taxicab to carry us to my apartment,
where you saw starlings bouncing across the sky.

I named you for the sun, for lions and eagles,
for everything you were not born with.

We slept in that place for months, two green peas
in the fork of a tree, before we changed cities,

hunkered down in a a basement walkout that
had little to recommend it, except a backyard

where you stepped on grass, and were afraid.
You soon discovered other pleasures

you would practice for the rest of your life:
naps in the sink, coconut oil from the jar.

We lived with a man for a few years,
but you didn't like him, so we left.

I worked long hours to pay rent alone
on an overpriced condo; stashed spare

dollars in the vain hope of someday
buying you a home so vast you'd never

think of cages again. Vanity pays.
We met someone with a small dog

and the same plan, abandoned the city's trap
of glamour for a garden. You slept everywhere,

had a hundred beds, lapped liver paté.
When I worked, you squirmed into the

aperture between my leg and the chair's arm,
and purred. Appeased as I'd ever seen you.

I can say now that the end began
with you hiding in the linen closet,

pleading for extra food while butter
slipped from the roundness of your ribs.

Still you spent nights in the crook
of my right arm, chirped as soon as

I stirred in the morning. You would look up
from your washing to meet my eyes in the

mirror while I brushed my teeth.
Cancer comes for the clever, too, doesn't it?

I should have been born into a higher order,
six-winged among the seraphim, so I could

fly you across the water to the ends of grace.
I should have cast myself a necromancer

so I could bring you back.
Simple as I am, I could do nothing

but swim your withered body over the river
and leave you lifeless on the far shore.

I returned alone to join the lowly,
we who can only lead one another to our deaths.

EPIZOOTIC

We were only ever dust to the clock, which made its hands on our backs all the more galling. Time was a virus, got inside of us: caught ourselves counting, caught our cells counting themselves, dying for the pleasure of adding a new number. When we moved, everything moved with us because seconds are small and we were not. Like all the sand in the sea, we settle, just as you wanted. Our words are motes in this new air, nonsense against blended senses. The clock ticks and you hiss, *show don't tell.*

AND THEN THE DARKNESS TALKS BACK

Six feet, apart or under: pick your
preposition. Death is grinning out of
breath, cozying up to chalk circles
and ringing bells in parks. A locust cloud
interrupts your picnic; a spider, unseen,
devours a cricket. Rain is on the event
horizon — will it come before evening,
will it come as frogs? The glaring sun
says nothing one too many times.
A man falls in front of you, not quite
six feet away. He is a ruler that you
will measure as you step back, yielding
to outbreak data. Swiss misanthropist
now, violent science is a neutral border;
try to never get involved. At home you
see the man fall over and over again,
a dusty film reel that won't stop spinning.
You are willing to become the receiver
for a friend with too much to spill.
Safety is mediated by distance, plastic
and words that are not your own.
When the voice on the telephone clicks
silent, you hear the night and cough
a cobweb into your hand.

EXTREMOPHILE

i

Water enough to withstand boiling,
bear enough to outlast the frigidity of space:
not adapted to exploit these conditions
only to endure them; slow walking.

ii

If a caterpillar met a manatee
on the eve of the apocalypse
and schemed to outlast everything
but the sun, they would become a much
smaller creature than anyone expected.

iii

Creator of all things, incognito.
Tried to exert *their* will on it,
but it would not take the shape.
So tardigrade becomes retrograde,
desiccating into glass and then
waiting for resurrection.

SPHINX

Severed heads, open minds:
like forgetting in an age of information.
Electrodes to the temples, positive thinking:
happiness is the stasis of a closed system.

The action of a preservative is to impede
decay; you don't believe in anything,
so your emptiness has no half-life.

When anarchy breaks windows, who cleans
up the glass? Is a country still run by democracy
after four years of regret? There are more
questions than answers.

Lay open wounds to sunshine
and disinfectant, to nature unveiled,
to instinctive elaboration of a conundrum.
There are more problems than

solutions, but you did always love
a riddle.

QUADRATE

Suck on baked sugar cane
and the caramel settles like marrow
in the jaw. Taste new flavours.
Curiosity is a wonderful quality.
Latex stretches and flexes, recurved
pleasure into the hollow of tooth,
then the base of the neck. Anaconda
sidewinding to dot an *i* with its
body drive. Rubberneck the x-ray
and it will show you calories emptying
your little white houses like thieves. Shadow
inquisition with acumen and a peppermint string.
Curiosity is a wonderful quality
in composite.

WHO WILL SAVE US

Dogs? Our friends know the notes of each of Death's perfumes:
cancers, bombs, a virus in the lungs. *We listen, but still miss
the point.*

AI? Intelligent agents can teach themselves to write prescient
prescriptions. *They assist, waiting for doctors to prove them
right.*

Circles? Shapes have shifted from geometric subjects to arithmetic
lecturers, conducting mass classes in pandemic math. *We add or
subtract, circle back.*

Mannequins? They stand stiff, checkerboarded between us and
our hungry, exhaling enemies, like mediators or crossing guards.
Seating has never been more limited.

Horseshoe Crabs? Canaries of the sea have blood of blue milk
that is more delicate than human plasma, a perfect laboratory
for testing purity. *If they live, we live.*

Holy Water? Sometimes a gun is a blessing that will keep you
breathing. Sunday's mass delusion blooms. *Our rituals will not
be diluted.*

Ghosts? Up and down village streets go those bones made of
smoke, those scythes cut from silk, speaking to us in Latin
alliteration: memento mori. *We don't know why but we run.*

GOOD DEATH

Sometimes the dogs made
dying look easy,

mass grave too grim a term

for the infinite puppy
snuggle puddle.

It begs: saliva-covered joy,
paw in mouth,

a universe marrowed
            between the wound
                        and the bone.

Late at night, still life
in the metallic glint

of the cages and
the operating table

— I want to follow them;
                        instead, I go home

to the sleeping cats,
muzzles pointing
to the sky.

BONE MEAL

To subsist on air and light alone,
that's her new *skinny girl* goal.
Simpler than photosynthesis,
leaner than a sapling. If her

disappearing act happened on
stage, it would be called magic.
Her short shelf life, another spiraled
stare case, they'll click *like* to her

gradual fading away. Encase the
dream in bone and paralyze the egg,
weight on the end of a string
to catch fish. Her spine

struggles to keep its curve,
fossilizing like the skeleton
of a compsognathus. An archive
in amber, awful in its indefinite end,

grim in the certainty of
dissolution. The wall, her brittle
hands. Push her back into a tree,
a lack forced to infinity.

THE ETERNAL ZOO

Breakfast in gazelle fur;
arsenic in a cooling teacup.
Uneasy physiognomy pools
on a pillow, half-dreamt.
Nature morte in visible shapes,
on permanent display.

Rare and bloody no more,
flesh severs from feeling.
Fluffed tails move away from
the flock. Salty skin stretched
over a mount lowers a thin veil
between subject and object,

ensnaring the idea of animal.
Skeletal lines ache inside
polyurethane foam; a posed
and unperishable bliss. This
dermatomb is the perfect stasis
that cages aspire to create.

On exhibition are humanity's
ersatz transmutations. Mammals
and mundane birds reinterpret
the phoenix, rising out of the ash
of death into which they disappeared:
Life still vivid in the distance.

TAXIDERMIA

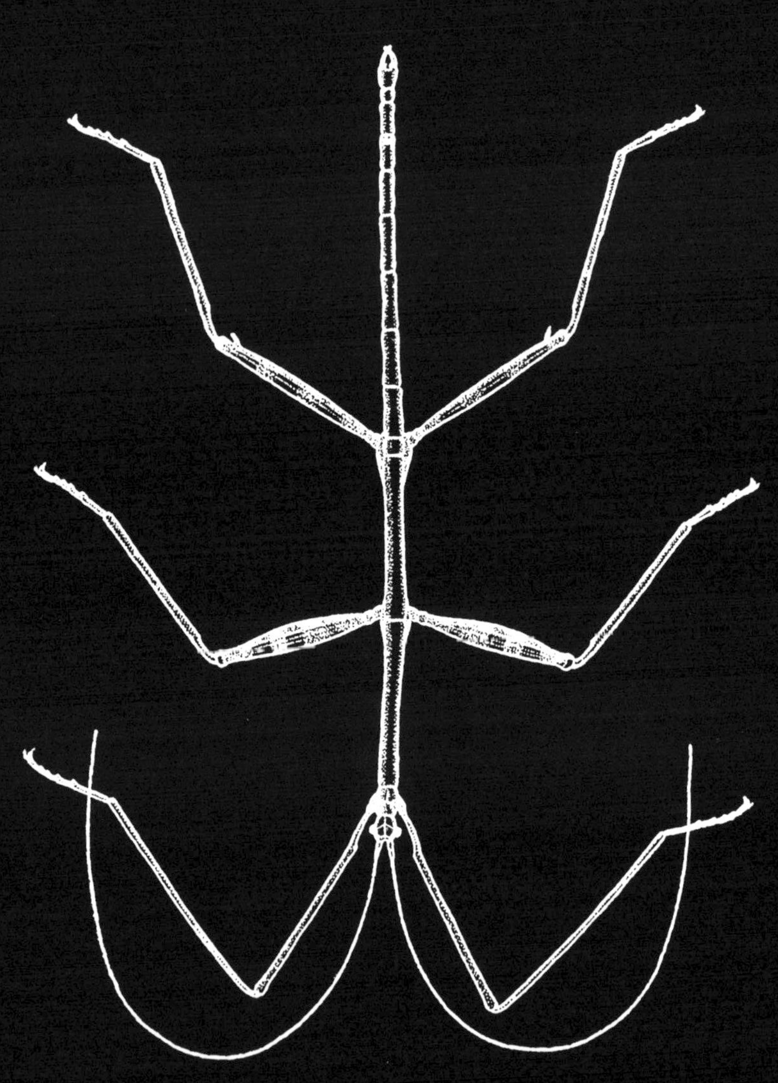

NOTES

The superb phrase "The Horse Eats No Cucumber Salad" is a translation of the first words successfully spoken over the 'telephon', a prototype electrical device invented by Germany's Johann Philipp Reis in 1861. Allegedly, the unusual and nonsensical phrase "Das Pferd frisst keinen Gurkensalat" was chosen as a test sentence for the machine because it could not be accurately guessed and would have to be heard clearly. Reis' device worked, but was unfortunately not embraced by the German scientific community; one noted physicist, J. C. Poggendorff, regarded the transmission of speech by electricity as a chimera. Alexander Graham Bell was officially awarded the first patent for the telephone in 1876, as he was able to produce a practical and commercially viable model.

Irv Teibel, via his company Syntonic Research Inc., produced the *environments* series of audio recordings between 1969 and 1979, which featured natural sounds (field recordings) without musical accompaniment. Miriam Berman, Syntonic's graphic designer, ma|de a three-panel comic that shows Teibel attempting to record the sound of a single snowflake. This was the point of departure for "Pitchdown Bay."

"The Extended Mourning of Orca *J35*" is about an orca whale, known as J35, or Tahlequah, who received international attention in 2018 when she carried the dead body of her second calf for more than two weeks, apparently out of grief. *Orcinus* is the genus, of which *Orcinus orca* is a member. The name *Orcinus* means, roughly, 'of the realms of the dead', after Orcus, the Roman god of the underworld. *Rostrum* refers to a whale's upper snout. *Epimeletic* refers to the behaviour of a healthy adult animal caring for a harmed or deceased animal, particularly a young one. Tahlequah did go on to have a third calf, who is reportedly still surviving.

"Ventral" is a work about sea angels. These visually alluring, shell-less sea snails are notable for their translucent skin — which allows for a clear view of their internal organs — and for their 'wings' (structures called parapodia) which rhythmically propel them through the open ocean, and give them the appearance of flying, creating an almost ethereal illusion. Carnivorous predators and protandrous hermaphrodites, they are also fascinating for many other reasons, some of which are alluded to in this work.

"Familiar" was composed as a sort of incantation, which gave us an excuse to play with rhyme in ways we normally shy away from; Robin Skelton's *Spellcraft: A Handbook of Invocations, Blessings, Protections, Healing Spells, Love Spells, Binding and Bidding* (McClelland and Stewart, 1978) served as a guide for our composition. The word *apotropaic* refers to a type of magic intended to ward off evil. There are several folkloric references in the poem to purported characteristics of animal familiars; for instance, that they were kept by witches in baskets lined with sheep's wool and fed items such as milk and meat.

"They Eat Them Weeping" references several anthropomorphic characters: boisterous Albert Alligator, from Walt Kelly's delightful *Pogo* comic strip; and happy-go-lucky Wally Gator, of the eponymous Hanna-Barbera TV series, which episodically chronicles his desire and efforts to escape the zoo where he lives. (Wally, incidentally, is also the name of a registered emotional support alligator for a Pennsylvania man in his sixties named Joie Henney).

"Narcomedusa" is a singular member of the order *Narcomedusae*, which includes several types of jellyfish.

"Interdominion" is a poem that springs forth from a dream Mark had of a spider crawling across ice. In case you were wondering: spiders can at times be active during the winter, and may even venture out onto frozen lakes, as envisioned. The imagistic ending of the poem alludes to the *Creazione di Adamo / Creation of Adam* Sistine Chapel ceiling fresco by Michaelangelo, and the title of the poem deliberately undermines a related verse from Genesis 1:26: "And God said, Let us make man in our image, after our likeness: and let them have dominion over the fish of the sea, and over the fowl of the air, and over the cattle, and over all the earth, and over every creeping thing that creepeth upon the earth."

“Vortext” is about multiple, unexplained disappearances of ships, planes and crews in Lake Michigan/*Mishigami*, in an area often referred to as the Lake Michigan Triangle, the name being an homage to the Bermuda Triangle. The poem also makes references to the alleged sea monster that lives in Lake Michigan, as well as the so-called Lake Michigan ‘Stonehenge,’ a line of stones over a mile in length on the lake bed. One of these stones is carved with what appears to be the image of a Mastodon, and it has been suggested that the stones could be a more than 10,000-year-old ‘drive line’ for herding caribou, according to underwater archaeologist Dr. Mark Holley.

Strictly speaking, the minimalist “Cryocaesura” is about bdelloid rotifers (also known as ‘wheel animals’), which are near-microscopic multicellular creatures that are particularly remarkable because they have been known to survive states of cryptobiosis — a type of dormancy in which an organism’s measurable metabolic processes temporarily stop — for tens of thousands of years. In 2021, scientists found 24,000-year-old specimens, which they unearthed from the Arctic permafrost via a drilling rig, and were actually able to revive. We imagined a creature in dormancy as a kind of caesura, a break or pause in the middle of the ordinary life cycle.

The title of “As the Next Day Dawned” is a translation from the Latin: *“Sequenti die aurora apparente,”* a phrase noteworthy for its appearance in a July 1098 letter by the crusader Anselm of Ribemont, the first known text to refer to Baphomet, supposed deity of the Knights Templar, also appearing in various occult and mystical traditions, often represented as a goat-headed man. The word *panic* is derived from Pan, the name of the Greek god of the wild who takes the form of a man with the hindquarters,

legs and horns of a goat. The Yule Goat, traditional in various Nordic countries and believed to be traceable to ancient Pagan festivals (according to the Carnegie Museum of Natural History), often appears today as either a Christmas ornament or a 40-foot-high outdoor figure shaped from straw and bound in red ribbons. In Norse mythology, the goat Heidrun eats of the tree Læraðr, often identified as Yggdrasil, an immense ash tree supposedly at the centre of the Nine Worlds of the cosmos. Reports of goats walking on two legs, often to compensate for injury, have appeared over the years across the globe.

"Menagerie" is titled in deference to the multiple meanings of the word: a collection of animals; an eclectic group of people; and, in the French word from which it derives *(ménage)*, housekeeping. *Severe clear* is an aviation phrase used to describe bright blue skies of unlimited visibility. Such conditions typically occur after a storm.

"No Performances Today" is a poem about Showmen's Rest, a section of Woodlawn Cemetery in Forest Park, Illinois, that is exclusively devoted to circus performers and roustabouts (workers who maintain a circus' animals, equipment and grounds). Showmen's Rest got its start as a mass grave for members of the Hagenbeck-Wallace Circus who were killed in the Hammond circus train wreck of June 22, 1918. Circuses had been making use of rail travel since 1854, and throughout the history of the U.S. circus, train wrecks caused many deaths, right up until 1994 when the last known fatal circus wreck took place in Lakeland, Florida. The Hammond circus train wreck of 1918 occurred at a rail station known as Ivanhoe Interlocking, and was first noticed by men stationed at the nearby Ivanhoe signal tower. The circus' animals, which typically travelled on a separate train ahead of the performers, were not injured in the wreck. In the weeks following the accident, victims were buried in Showmen's Rest, and more than 1500 mourners gathered to pay their respects. A number of stone elephants surround Showmen's Rest, with their trunks lowered to symbolize mourning.

"Death Goes Green" was a phrase that appeared on the March 2016 cover of *The Walrus*, in reference to environmentally-friendly methods for managing corpses.

"Vorescape" is for Marcos Rodríguez Pantoja, of Spain.

The title "Organon Unravelling" refers to *organon* in its general sense, as an instrument of thought or a system of logic.

"Zoomorphs" and "Furverts" are meant to be read as a set, both approaching the subject of the furry fandom from different, and equally serious,

perspectives. Despite the fact that "Furverts" is written in first person plural, the authors cannot claim any personal experience with this subject area. We are indebted, among other sources, to the 2020 documentary *The Fandom* for the information upon which these poems were based. The phrase "forest of illusion" in "Furverts" alludes to the Forest of Illusion group responsible for preserving old Nintendo video games, one of which was *Dinosaur Planet*, from the creators of *Star Fox*, the latter of which is often credited with drawing many furries into the fandom. The final lines of "Furverts" allude to David Cory's *Little Jack Rabbit and the Circus Elephant* (Grosset & Dunlap Inc., 1928).

The rook in "Vertical Logic at the Crossroads of the World" bears a passing resemblance to Sylvia Plath's bird in "Black Rook in Rainy Weather."

"Subsidized Housing for Small Birds" borrows phrases from George H. Harrison's *The Backyard Bird Watcher: The Classic Guide to Enjoying Wild Birds Outside Your Back Door* (Simon & Schuster Inc., 1988). The noise a kestrel makes has been described as *'kee-kee-kee.'* The word *syrinx*, which refers to the vocal organ of birds, is from the Greek word for pan pipes. According to the study "The limits of egg recognition: testing acceptance thresholds of American robins in response to decreasingly egg-shaped objects in the nest" by Mark E. Hauber, Sarah K. Winnicki, Jeffrey P. Hoover,

Daniel Hanley and Ian R. Hays (*Royal Society Open Science*, 2021), robins are more likely to reject 'egg-shaped models' the thinner and more angular they become. A birding hotline is a telephone number that birders can call to get a taped listing of unusual species recently seen in the area.

"Panopticondominium" is, of course, a portmanteau of *Panopticon + condominium*, a freshly coined word that is so imagistic and ominous that we wish we had the extra funds sitting around to trademark it today; we're dreading the day when an opportunistic novelist or filmmaker runs it into the mainstream without an appropriate credit or royalty (please take note: *we will sue*).

"Arbeitslied" is a German word that translates to 'work song.' In the study "Singing in a Silent Spring: Birds Respond to a Half-Century Soundscape Reversion during the COVID-19 Shutdown" (*Science*, 2020), researchers Michael J. Blum, Elizabeth P. Derryberry, Graham E. Derryberry, David Luther and Jennifer N. Phillips found that a reduction in traffic noise enabled male white-crowned sparrows in San Francisco to sing songs in a different frequency, which was more attractive to females. Similarly, traffic noise has been found to negatively affect the mating choices of the two-spotted cricket, leading to nonoptimal mate selection, according to the study "Anthropogenic Noise Disrupts Mate Choice Behaviors in Female *Gryllus Bimaculatus*" (*Behavioural Ecology*, 2021) by Adam M. Bent, Thomas C. Ings and Sophie L. Mowles. Researchers Koki Tsujii, Tomonari Akamatsu, Ryosuke Okamoto, Kyoichi Mori, Yoko Mitani and Naoya Umeda found that humpback whales are less likely to sing at all when shipping noise is present, as reported in the study "Change in singing behavior of humpback whales caused by shipping noise" (*PLOS*, 2018).

"Apocalypse Parrot Screams for Vengeance" is a noisy little text containing many sonic references: it most strongly evokes *Hatebeak*, a death metal act featuring Waldo, a grey parrot (allegedly the first band to have an avian vocalist); 'His Master's Voice,' a phrase coined in the late 1890s, originally the title of an 1898 painting depicting a terrier-mix named Nipper tilting his head while listening to a cylinder phonograph, which was later modified to show the dog listening to a wind-up disc gramophone and adopted as a famous trademark and logo of the Victor Talking Machine Company, later known as RCA Victor; Ozzy Osbourne, who onced worked as a horn tester in a car factory; *death growl*, a vocal technique used in various heavy metal styles; the Latin phrase *malum in se*, which means 'evil in itself'; and, *membrana tympaniformis*, which refers to the walls of a bird's syrinx.

"Sky Bird" is a poem about man's preoccupation with flight and flying. The common cruising altitude for most commercial airplanes is between 33,000 and 42,000 feet, or between about six and nearly eight miles above sea level.

The basic frame of "Sugarwhip" is the 'carrot-and-stick' metaphor of reward and punishment as a way to induce a desired behaviour, which drew our attention because it relies on assumptions about a hierarchical power dynamic between the human driving the cart and the animal pulling it, though the implications of the metaphor are applied to both human and animal subjects. The poem's title plays on the German idiom 'sugar bread and whip,' which is said to be a variation or translation of 'carrot and stick'.

The line *"Would you mind if I tagged along with you?"* in "Wrecked by a Cloud" was something Jade said to Mark in reference to an event at Toronto's Royal Cinema called *Women Synth Pioneers: A Life In Waves & The Delian Mode*. This would have been their first date, if Jade had not cancelled due to a work-related court appearance; instead, the social coupling took place two days later at *Paperbacks from Hell Live,* a Grady Hendrix lecture hosted by The Miskatonic Institute of Horror Studies.

In "Psychopomp," the phrase "*Animal Sola*" is a play on the Catholic concept of *Anima Sola*, or 'lonely soul,' which is applied to souls in purgatory. The phrase "fallen giant" refers to the Nephilim of the Hebrew Bible: the word *Nephilim* has been variously translated as 'giants' or 'fallen angels,' who have sometimes been construed as existing between humanity and divinity. *Seraphim*, by contrast, are unambiguously high-ranking heavenly beings. The titular word *psychopomp* refers to a variety of creatures, spirits, angels or deities responsible for guiding the deceased from Earth to the afterlife.

"Extremophile" is about tardigrades (also known as 'water bears' or 'moss piglets'), some species of which are nearly indestructible multi-cellular micro-animals, able to live in all parts of Earth's biosphere, and even to survive exposure to outer space. Astrophysicists have predicted that these species of tardigrades will likely persist as long as the Earth and the Sun do, except in the highly improbable case that all of Earth's water evaporates. The tardrigrades would be able to withstand various apocalyptic events, such as asteroids, supernovae and gamma ray bursts, that would destroy most other life forms. Their remarkable endurance is largely the result of cryptobiosis — an ability to lose as much as ninety-seven percent of the water in their body and go dormant, sometimes for decades.

"Sphinx" alludes to something Justin Trudeau said in March 2017 in the House of Commons in support of Iqra Khalid's private member's motion 103, a non-binding motion condemning Islamophobia and religious discrimination and calling on the government to develop a government-wide approach to reducing systemic racism and religious discrimination. Trudeau said, *"We need to [...] lay open wounds to sunshine and disinfectant. That is also the role that we have in this House and that we have as active, engaged citizens in this country."*

Since it has been asked before regarding "Quadrate," we will clarify: anacondas have been observed to sidewind, but rarely. Such behaviour was, for example, described by W. G. Ryerson and S. Horwitz in a 2014 article for the *Herpetological Review*.

"Who Will Save Us" refers to several early, proposed pre-vaccine interventions or treatments to address the COVID-19 pandemic.

"Good Death," titled for the Greek root of the word *euthanasia*, was written in awareness of the fact that veterinarians have been reported to be more than twice as likely to be suicidal or to die by suicide than Canadians in other job classes. Suicidality among vets has been attributed to high debt loads, as well as stressful work, due in no small part to having to euthanize their patients, a job that doctors, by contrast, perform far less often, if at all.

The title of "The Eternal Zoo" comes from a misremembering of the title of Rachel Poliquin's book *The Breathless Zoo* (subtitled *Taxidermy and the Culture of Longing*, Penn State University Press, 2012). Our poem makes reference to Méret Oppenheim's artwork *Le Déjeuner en fourrure / The Luncheon in Fur*, a fur-covered teacup, saucer and spoon, which the MoMA describes as "perhaps the single most notorious Surrealist object." The poem also alludes to Damien Hirst's artwork *Away from the Flock*, in which a dead sheep is suspended in formaldehyde and displayed in a glass tank; it was one of Hirst's earliest taxidermy-adjacent works. The phrase *nature morte* refers to what is known in English as *still life*. We use *physiognomy* here in its most general sense: making inferences about the nature or character of a thing based on its external appearance.

The poems (1) "Milkweed," (2) "Metempsychosis," (3) "Minikin" and (4) "Michoacán" constitute the "Monarch Suite." Collectively, these poems detail the complex life cycle and migratory patterns of monarch butterflies (*Danaus plexippus*) — from the beginning of their life as gorging milkweed caterpillars; to the transformative, speculative mysteries which occur inside the chrysalis; back out into their impressive journey across thousands of kilometres toward overwintering sites; ending in the mountains of Mexico, where they hibernate in enormous clusters in the branches of perfectly chosen trees, the exact same trees that were visited by their ancestors in previous years.

Because of its long travels and wide distribution, the monarch butterfly is also sometimes referred to as 'The Wanderer'. Fittingly, the achronological ordering of the texts that make up this suite allows their poetic narrative to roam through our pages, while simultaneously conforming to the ascending sections of the book, which are ordered beginning with the sea (the likely origin of life on earth), moving onto land, up into the sky and continually rising toward the nebulous metaphysical sphere.

Sweetwater sea is a term sometimes used to refer to the Great Lakes; we were introduced to it by artist Rod Strickland through his exhibition "Around the Sweet Sea" (Art Gallery of Windsor, 1990).

There is no known original source for the Werner Herzog epigraph in the "WATER" section. The Alice Walker epigraph in "LAND" comes from her preface to *The Dreaded Comparison: Human and Animal Slavery* (New Society Publishers, 1988) by Marjorie Spiegel. The William Blake epigraph in "AIR" comes from *The Marriage of Heaven and Hell* (John W. Luce and Company, 1906). The Antonio Porchia epigraph in "ELSEWHERE" comes from *Voices* (Copper Canyon Press, 2003), translated by W. S. Merwin.

ACKNOWLEDGEMENTS

Firstly, our heartfelt thanks to editor Jim Johnstone for believing in this project, in both form and content! You've been supportive and generous throughout, kindly allowing us the space to shape this book to match our vision.

Many thanks to the entire Palimpsest Press team, including publisher Aimée Parent Dunn and publicist Vanessa Shields, for all their help readying this collection to meet the world. We owe a debt of gratitude as well to Rachel Poliquin, and the team of Gary Barwin and Tom Prime, for their endorsements of *ZZOO*.

A huge thank you to Andy Verboom, publisher of *long con magazine* and Collusion Books, for promoting and valorizing the art of collaboration, including our work and writing. Collusion published *A Trip to the ZZOO*, a chapbook which directly led to the development of this manuscript; that chapbook was shortlisted for the 2021 bpNichol Chapbook Award. Thank you also to the Meet the Presses collective for facilitating that award, and to its 2021 jurors, Jordan Abel and Jennifer Lovegrove.

We would also like to warmly thank Jeremy Colangelo, Hollay Ghadery, Rob McLennan, Michael Russell, Kevin Spenst and Bryce Warnes for reviewing and championing our early work; Priscilla Brett, Jordan Fry, Daniel & Emily Lockhart and Monty Reid for giving us opportunities to share and discuss our collaborative practice; Louis Cabri, Karl Jirgens, Charlie Lucas, Conor McDonnell, Maria Meindl, James Millhaven, Samuel Strathman and Laurie Wallace for their sustained engagement, encouragement and kind words.

Mark would like to personally thank Julie Cameron Gray, Daniel Scott Tysdal and Catriona Wright for participating in conversations/explorations back in spring 2017 related to the ill-fated project *The Conductor*, which importantly revealed the possibilities and limitations of collaborative authorship.

Immense gratitude to the Canada Council for the Arts for supporting the development of this collection. Our sincere appreciation to the Ontario Arts Council — as well as Brick Books, *Hamilton Arts & Letters* magazine and Guernica Editions, for funding production of this work through the OAC's Recommender Grants for Writers program.

Poems from *ZZOO* have previously appeared in the following publications:

- *Antilang*: "Flashback to the Crab Nebula" and "Panopticondominium" — published by Jordan Bolay and Allie McFarland
- *The Chachalaca Review* (US): "Epizootic" — edited by Regina L. Lien
- *Grey Borders Magazine*: "Crossing the Date Line," "Organon Unravelling," "Sphinx," "Splice / Stitch" and "We Must Be Thankful for the Truth" — published by Priscilla Brett and Jordan Fry
- *Guttural* (UK): "Extremophile," "Minimal Surfaces" and "When We Were Wolves" — edited by Nathan Hassall and Gemma Jackson

- *NōD Magazine*: "Blue Sunlight" — edited by Kat Heger

- *The Pine Cone Review* (US): "And Then The Darkness Talks Back" (nominated for a 2021 Best of the Net Award) and "Who Will Save Us" — edited by Susmita Paul

- *Poetry Is Dead*: "Apocalypse Parrot Screams for Vengeance" — guest edited by Carleigh Baker and David James Brock

- *PRISM International*: "Bone Meal" — edited by Jessica Johns

- *Rat's Ass Review* (US): "Vertical Logic at the Crossroads of the World" — edited by Roderick Bates

- *Savant-Garde*: "The Extended Mourning of Orca *J35*" — published by Amélie Robitaille

- *Tiny Spoon* (US): "They Eat Them Weeping" — edited by C. M. Chady and Stephanie Hempel

- *Trinity Review*: "Nerve Bouquet" — edited by Grace Ma and Usman Malik

- *Vallum*: "Pitchdown Bay" — edited by Leigh Kotsilidis

- "Death Goes Green" — anthologized in *Is This a Good Time* (Collusion Books, 2020)

THIS BOOK
IS DEDICATED TO:

Sylvie Bélanger, Fred Gaysek, David Haskins, John Scott, R. M. Vaughan — dearly departed friends and teachers

Ari and *Mandy* — delightful companion animals who are always still quietly present

We miss you.

First Edition.
Spring, 2025

ISBN 978-1-990293-85-6

Printed and bound in Canada

Cover available in
FOXHOLE, TANNIAN,
SERPENTINE, INSECTOID and
COSMICIST variants

PALIMPSEST PRESS
1171 Eastlawn Ave
Windsor, ON / N8S 3J1
CANADA

info@palimpsestpress.ca
palimpsestpress.ca

MA|DE (est. 2018) is a collaborative writing entity, a unity of two voices fused into a single, poetic third. It is the name given to the joint authorship of **Mark Laliberte** and **Jade Wallace** — artists whose active solo practices, while differing radically, serve to complement one another. **MA|DE**'s work together is often exploratory in nature, formulating a set of shared visions, symbols and ciphers that invite the reader into their complex, continually-expanding internal universe. **MA|DE**'s writing has appeared in numerous journals and chapbooks, and they have delivered workshops on collaborative writing at several festivals, including VerseFest Ottawa. With the support of the Ontario Arts Council and the Canada Council for the Arts, they completed their debut full-length collection, ***ZZOO***, and their follow-up, ***Alphabeticals,*** and are currently working on three new, creatively divergent manuscripts: ***Detourism***, ***Twin Visible*** and ***Waste Not the Marrow***.

Chapbooks

Test Centre (2019)

A Trip to the ZZOO (2020)

A Barely Concealed Design (2020)

Expression Follows Grim Harmony (2023)

ma-de.ca

My new girlfriend works at the zoo; I think she's a keeper.

OUR

RABBLE

OF

RABBITS

GO

NIBBLING

ON

RIBBONS